MEET THE STEGOSAURUS

Fun Facts & Cool Pictures

Julian Hawking

Table of Contents

Meet the Stegosaurus: The Dinosaur with a Small Brain

Just as you and your friends are all different, dinosaurs also have features that distinguish them from other types of dinosaurs. For the Stegosaurus, it was the large plates positioned along the back that made them stand out from others walking the earth during the Jurassic period. These plates are the reason this dinosaur was named Stegosaurus. This name means roof lizard or covered lizard.

Stegosaurus dinosaurs probably weren't the smartest animals wandering the earth, so they had to be among the best armed. Their bodies were covered in natural weapons of self-defense that provided them some protection from the many meat-eating dinosaurs wandering the earth during their lifetime. Keep reading to learn about this unique dinosaur's strange body and how it impacted the dinosaur's way of life.

When the Stegosaurus Walked the Earth

Stegosaurus walked the earth toward the end of the Jurassic period. This was approximately 150 million years ago, and there were many dinosaurs on the earth at that time. During the Jurassic period, the earth was warm and sunny. There was a lot of water, and flooded areas were scattered across the map. Fresh green vegetation grew all over the earth, so the

Stegosaurus would have been able to find delicious plants to eat without a problem.

It was at the end of the Jurassic period that most dinosaurs became extinct. This means that they disappeared from the earth and no longer existed as they had before. Scientists continue to debate what could have happened to these dinosaurs. The Stegosaurus was one type of dinosaur that became extinct during this period.

Picture the Stegosaurus

When you think about dinosaurs, you might assume that everything about them was enormous. That was not always true, and the Stegosaurus is a great example. This dinosaur had an unusually small head that came to a point, much like the beak of a bird.

What were large about the Stegosaurus were the flat plates positioned along its back and down its tail. These plates were shaped like triangles and covered the back much like shingles cover the roof of a house. Since blood vessels ran throughout these plates, they were likely used to help the dinosaur maintain a comfortable body temperature, since they lived outdoors without protection from the weather. All Stegosaurus had 17 plates, and each plate measured 2.5 feet wide and 2.5 feet tall.

The Stegosaurus also had a large tail. The tail had spikes measuring four feet long and was used as a weapon for self-defense. Other animals that chose to attack this type of dinosaur would have been whipped with a strong, spiked tail designed to cause injury. Due to the length of its tail, the length of the whole Stegosaurus body measured up to 30 feet. Scientists believe they were approximately 9 feet tall.

The Stegosaurus had four legs, but the back legs were much taller than the front legs. Scientists believe that the dinosaur walked on all four legs, but the shorter front legs made them move a bit differently than other dinosaurs. The front legs had five little toes, and the back legs had three little toes.

Stegosaurus in Action

Next time you see someone moping along slowly with their eyes turned down to the ground, think of the Stegosaurus. This dinosaur was known to carry its head down toward the ground, so the rest of its body would have been up higher than its head most of the time. Scientists believe that it may have never taken its head more than three feet above the ground. This body posture was natural to the Stegosaurus because of its short front legs.

Many dinosaurs could stand upright on their back two legs, but scientists are uncertain whether the Stegosaurus could do that. If this dinosaur had to stay down on all four legs, its range of motion would have been restricted. It would not have been able to reach for food in trees or high bushes, and it would have been at a disadvantage in fights with taller animals.

The Stegosaurus was at even more of a disadvantage in fights because it moved so slowly. It could not match the fast motions of other animals or run away when under attack. This may be why the Stegosaurus was naturally covered in its armor of spikes, plates, and scales.

Stegosaurus Senses: What Were Its Strengths?

Its sense of smell was the Stegosaurus' greatest strength. It needed this sense in order to detect fresh vegetation and determine what fruits were ripe and ready to eat. This dinosaur may not have had the brain power to solve second-grade math problems, but it would have been able to put together a fresh salad with a side of fruit faster than any modern-day chef who was forced to live out in the wild.

What's for Dinner?

The Stegosaurus had limited food options because they didn't have large teeth. Their teeth were small and were positioned farther up in their cheeks rather than right inside the opening of their mouths. They didn't have the powerful teeth needed to chew up other animals, so they naturally turned to plants and other soft foods that they could chew easily with less tooth power.

Since this type of dinosaur only ate plants, it is known as an herbivore. Since there were many larger dinosaurs alive during the Jurassic period and most of them ate animals, it is likely that the Stegosaurus had to defend itself regularly to prevent becoming another dinosaur's dinner.

Would you ever eat a side of pebbles with your salad? The Stegosaurus is believed to have eaten small rocks along with its fresh vegetation. It is possible that the rocks helped the dinosaur break down the plants so that the food could pass through the body.

Would a Stegosaurus Want to Be Your Friend?

Scientists believe that the Stegosaurus might have been a social animal. They study the remains of these animals that have been found in order to determine how close they may have been to other animals. From the remains found to date, it is believed that Stegosaurus may have traveled in groups. Many other types of animals have shown no signs of traveling together, so if you ever wanted to make friends with a dinosaur, this might have been one of the friendliest.

What the Stegosaurus Left Behind

Photo by EvaK

In 1992, a paleontologist (a scientist who studies animal remains) in Colorado came across the remains of a Stegosaurus and clearly identified the arrangement of the plates stretching across its back and down its tail. Remains found previously also had these plates, but this finding revealed that the plates were positioned in two distinct rows rather than being scattered without a pattern.

Photo by Thomas Quine

This finding in Colorado also revealed large scales covering the neck and hip area of the Stegosaurus. These scales are believed to have protected the dinosaur when in fights. It is not certain whether all Stegosaurus had these scales or not.

Photo by terren in Virginia

The very first Stegosaurus remains were found in Colorado in 1876, but many other fossils have been found throughout the Western United States, Europe, India, China, and Africa. We know a lot about this dinosaur because so many fossil remains have been discovered.

Weird Stegosaurus Facts

- "You have a brain the size of a pea!" This is a common insult that humans use, but it applies perfectly to the

Stegosaurus. Since they had small heads, they naturally had small brains. Their brains were a bit larger than a pea, but not much larger than a walnut.

• The first Stegosaurus dinosaurs to walk the earth were believed to have spikes on their shoulders for added self-protection. Stegosaurus living later in the Jurassic period were missing these shoulder spikes.

• What does a horse have in common with a Stegosaurus? Each of the Stegosaurus' toes had a tiny hoof, kind of like the larger hooves of the horses we know today. These hooves protected the dinosaur's toes so that it could run and walk without pain.

Stegosaurus in Our World Today

Photo by Piotrus

The Stegosaurus is the state dinosaur of Colorado due to the number of Stegosaurus fossils found in that state. This is one of the most well-known dinosaurs today, and it is often the type of dinosaur used for children's toys. You can even find toy Stegosaurus dinosaurs that walk by remote control. You can also find Transformer toys and cartoons that feature creatures that are able to transform into a Stegosaurus.

Photo by Jakub Halun

You can also find the Stegosaurus featured in many movies. It first appeared in the original version of King Kong and was also featured in Steven Spielberg's film The Lost World. Perhaps the cutest Stegosaurus in our world today is Spike from The Land before Time.

Other Books In This Series

Did you know that there are other dinosaur books in this series that you might enjoy?

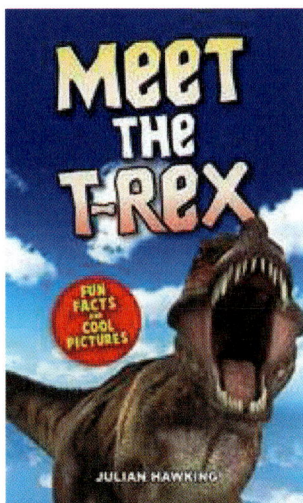

Meet The T-Rex

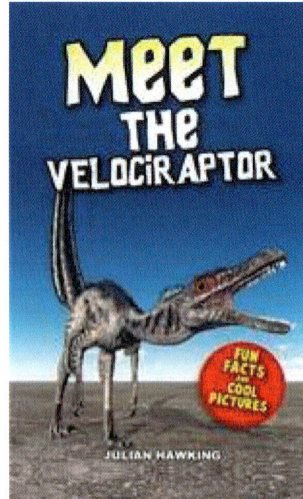

Meet The Velociraptor

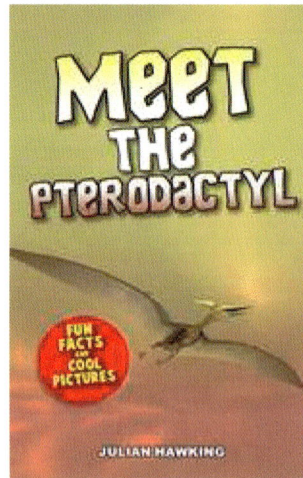

Meet The Pterodactyl

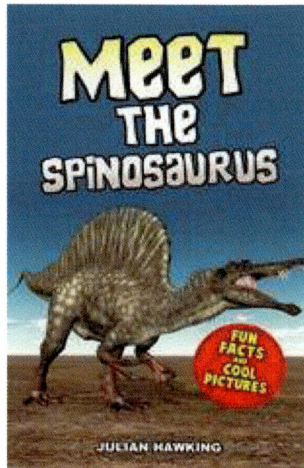

Meet The Spinosaurus

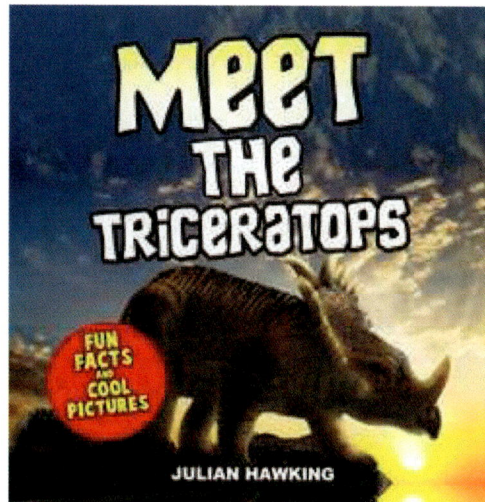

Meet The Triceratops

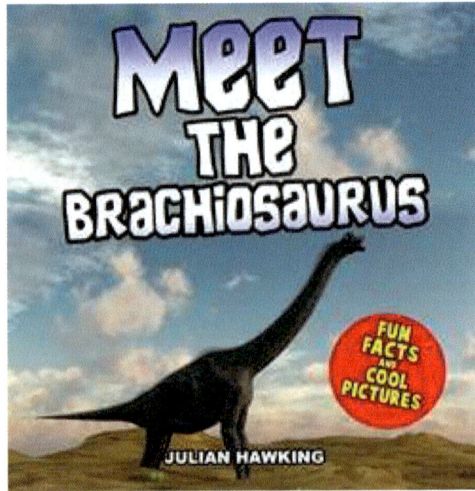

Meet The Brachiosaurus

10038828R00022

Printed in Great Britain
by Amazon.co.uk, Ltd.,
Marston Gate.